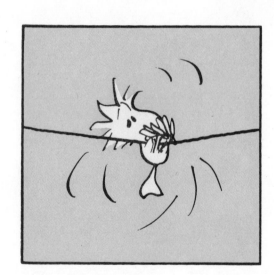

CHARLIE BROWN'S
'CYCLOPEDIA

Super Questions and Answers and Amazing Facts

Featuring
Electricity and Magnetism

VOLUME
15

THIS BOOK
BELONGS TO

Jenny

Based on the Charles M. Schulz Characters

Funk & Wagnalls, Inc.

Photograph and Illustration credits: American Telephone & Telegraph Company, 669, 702, 708; Bell Laboratories, 701, 702; Consolidated Edison Company of New York, Inc., 678; Fundamental Photographs, 675, 690, 717; Ray-O-Vac, a Corporation of INCO Electro-Energy, 699; Scientific Atlanta, 707; Smithsonian Institution Photo No. Edison 51144, 692; Tennessee Valley Authority, 683.

1 2 3 4 5 6 7 8 9 0

A large part of this volume was previously published in *Charlie Brown's Fifth Super Book of Questions and Answers.*

Introduction

Welcome to volume 15 of *Charlie Brown's 'Cyclopedia*! Have you ever wondered how a doorbell works, or what a watt is, or why batteries go dead? Charlie Brown and the rest of the *Peanuts* gang are here to help you find the answers to these questions and many more about electricity and magnetism. Have fun!

Electricity and Magnetism

What is electricity?

Electricity is a kind of energy. In order to understand how this energy is created, you have to know something about atoms. Atoms are the tiny, tiny bits of matter that all things are made of. Atoms are so small that you can't see them even with the most powerful microscope. Though atoms are so small, they are made of even smaller parts. Some of these parts are called electrons (ih-LECK-tronz). Electrons cause electricity.

When electrons move around among the atoms of matter, there is a current of electricity. In some materials, the electrons are loosely attached to the atoms. This makes it easy to break the electrons loose and have them move to other atoms. Electrons are loosely attached in all metals. That is why people use metal wires to carry electricity from one place to another. We say that these wires are good "conductors," or carriers, of electricity.

What is a magnet?

A magnet is something that can attract iron. A very simple magnet may be a bar of iron or steel. Sometimes the bar is bent into the form of a horseshoe.

A magnet's attraction is strongest at its ends, or poles. Every magnet has a north pole and a south pole. If you hold two magnets near each other, the north pole of one will be attracted to the south pole of the other. If you try to bring the north pole of one magnet together with the north pole of another, they will push apart, or repel, each other. This also happens with two south poles. Opposite poles attract each other. Poles of the same kind repel.

What do magnets have to do with electricity?

A lot. Magnetism and electricity are close relatives. In fact, electricity can produce magnetism. And magnetism can produce electricity.

A magnet has an invisible field, or cloud, of magnetic force around it. A wire with electricity running through it has the same kind of invisible magnetic field around it.

You can show the shape of a magnet's invisible field. Put a magnet under a piece of paper. Then sprinkle powdered iron on top of the paper.

674

Do some magnets run on electricity?

Yes. They are called electromagnets. You can make a small electromagnet by winding lots of thin copper wire around an iron nail. Use wire that has a protective covering. Scrape off about an inch of the covering at each end of the wire. Attach the ends to a battery, as in the picture. An electric current flows from the battery through the wire to the nail. And the nail becomes magnetic. It can pick up other iron things. If you disconnect the wire from the battery, the nail loses almost all of its magnetism.

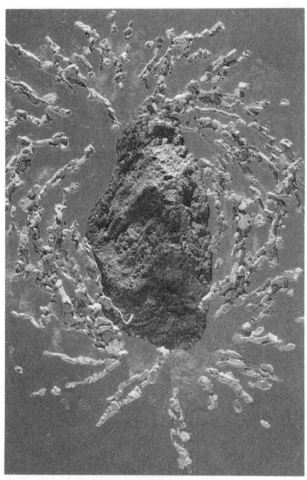

Colored iron filings show magnetic field around piece of magnetite

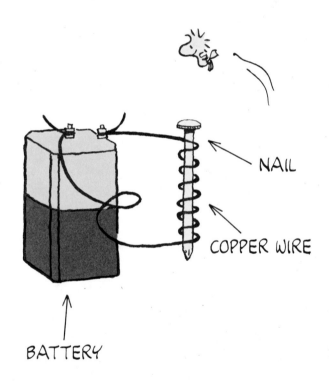

NAIL

COPPER WIRE

BATTERY

 The world's biggest magnet is 196 feet (59 meters) across and weighs 40,000 tons!

675

Are electromagnets better than ordinary magnets?

In at least one way, yes. An electromagnet works only when it is turned on. So with an electromagnet you can lift a heavy iron object and move it to any place you want. As soon as you shut off the electricity, the electromagnet will stop working. It will drop the iron at the place you choose.

You could not do this with an ordinary magnet. An ordinary magnet keeps holding on to iron things. That's why it is sometimes called a permanent magnet. "Permanent" means lasting forever. If you want to separate a piece of iron from a permanent magnet, you must pull it off.

How are electromagnets used?

Big electromagnets are often used in junkyards to load scrap iron into railroad cars. They are also used to separate iron from other kinds of scrap, such as aluminum or copper or glass. Small electromagnets are used to make some machines work. For example, a doorbell uses an electromagnet.

How does a doorbell work?

When you push the button outside a door, electricity goes through wires to a small electromagnet in the doorbell. The magnet pulls on a flat steel spring. The spring is attached to a little hammer that hits the bell. But as soon as the spring moves and the hammer hits the bell, the electric flow, or current, shuts off. This is because the spring's movement pulled apart two pieces of metal that were touching. The current can't flow unless these two pieces of metal touch each other. When the current stops, the spring bounces back to its original position. Now the two pieces of metal that were apart are touching each other again. So the current flows again. And the electromagnet pulls the spring to make the hammer strike the bell again. As long as you keep your finger on the button, the spring will keep flipping back and forth very fast. And the bell will keep on ringing.

A doorbell works by pushing a button — unless of course you have a door knocker. In that case you have a problem.

Sally Brown

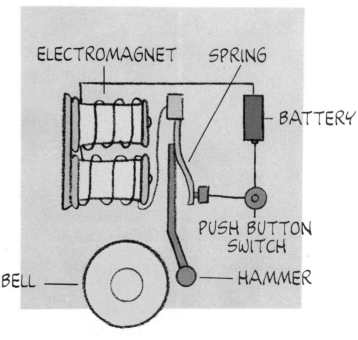

BATTERY-OPERATED DOORBELL

ELECTROMAGNET   SPRING   BATTERY
PUSH BUTTON SWITCH
BELL   HAMMER

677

Where do electric currents come from?

Most of the electric currents that people use come from batteries or from machines called generators. The current that runs the lights, the toaster, the refrigerator, and other things in your house probably comes from a very large generator in a place called a power plant.

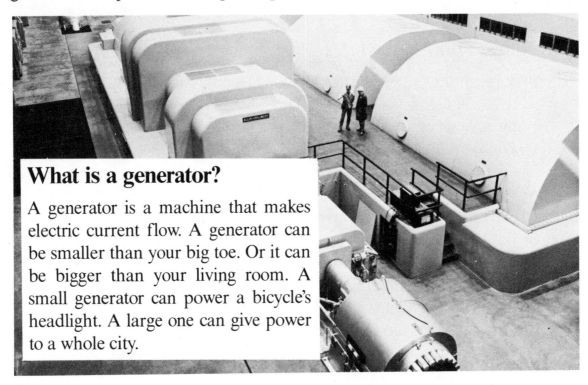

What is a generator?

A generator is a machine that makes electric current flow. A generator can be smaller than your big toe. Or it can be bigger than your living room. A small generator can power a bicycle's headlight. A large one can give power to a whole city.

How does a generator produce an electric current?

A generator changes one kind of energy into another. Every generator is run by something that turns or spins. The turning wheel of a bicycle runs the generator that powers its headlight. The spinning wheels or blades of a large engine run the generator that produces electric power for a city. In the generator, the spinning energy is turned into electric energy. Here's how.

The people who make generators keep certain scientific facts in mind:

1. Around every magnet are invisible lines of force.   2. If you move a coil of copper wire past a magnet, the wire cuts across the lines of force.
3. When the lines of force are cut by the wire, electricity flows through the wire.

Inside a generator are magnets (often electromagnets) and a coil of wire. The wire is usually around a rod called an armature (ARM-uh-choor). The engine that runs the generator moves the armature. As long as the armature keeps moving, the magnets' lines of force are cut. As long as the magnets' lines of force are cut, a current of electricity is produced, or generated.

What is a battery?

A battery is something that generates an electric current by chemical reaction. A chemical reaction may take place when chemicals mix together and change into other chemicals.

You've probably seen the battery that is inside a portable radio or a flashlight. It looks something like a small can. This can and everything inside it is called a dry cell. Some batteries are made up of one dry cell. Others use two or more. Inside dry cells are all the chemicals and other things needed to produce electric current.

The chemicals in dry cells are in the form of jellies or pastes. They can't be spilled. That's why these cells are called dry cells. There are also cells called wet cells. The chemicals inside these are liquids. Some batteries called storage batteries can be recharged and used over and over again. One kind of storage battery is used to start a car. It is made of three or six cells in a plastic box.

Most batteries come in standard sizes and shapes. Some tiny ones are used to run watches. Some huge ones are used to run submarines.

Batteries

The world's oldest working battery is in a laboratory in England. It has been generating a tiny current of electricity since 1840!

How does a battery produce an electric current?

Batteries produce currents by chemical reaction. Usually, a cell of a battery has three chemicals. One, called the electrolyte (ih-LECK-troe-lite), causes the other two to react. When the two chemicals react, the electrons in their atoms do a lot of moving around. One chemical ends up with a load of extra electrons. Another chemical ends up with a shortage of electrons. In this way, these two chemicals become what is called electrically charged. The chemical with extra electrons gets a negative or minus charge. The chemical with a shortage of electrons gets a positive or plus charge. When the chemicals are electrically charged, the electricity is ready to flow out of the battery.

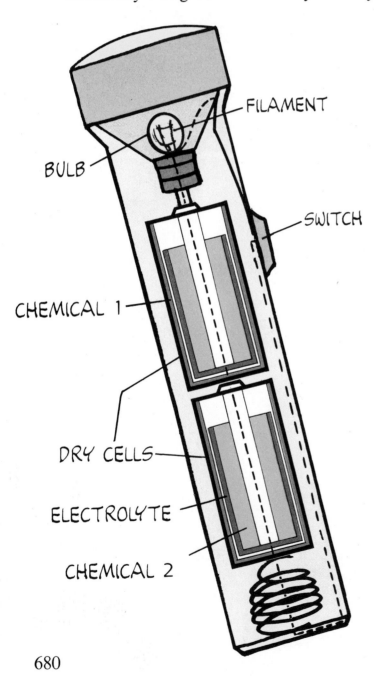

FILAMENT

BULB

SWITCH

CHEMICAL 1

DRY CELLS

ELECTROLYTE

CHEMICAL 2

In order for the flow to begin, there must be a complete path for the current to follow. Such a path is called an electric circuit (SIR-kit). The electrons move around the circuit by using energy given to them by the battery. Suppose the circuit is in a flashlight. As the electrons move along, they change electric energy to heat energy and light energy. And the bulb lights up.

What makes batteries go dead?

When a battery can no longer produce current, we say it is dead. A battery stops producing all current when its chemical reaction stops. The reaction stops when some of the chemicals have been used up. That means the chemicals have changed into other chemicals.

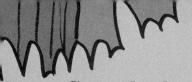

Can a dead or weak battery be made to work like new again?

Ordinary flashlight batteries can't be renewed, but certain other batteries can. These are called storage batteries. Renewing a battery is called recharging it. Cars have rechargeable batteries. Some electric drills, small vacuum cleaners, and electronic calculators run on rechargeable batteries.

How are car batteries recharged?

Car batteries recharge automatically when the car's engine is running. The engine is connected to a generator. The generator forces a current to run backward through the battery. This means the new chemicals change back into the old chemicals. The chemicals can react again to generate more electricity. Recharging is what allows the battery to keep starting the car every day for years.

HERE'S THE WORLD FAMOUS BEAGLE SCOUT LEADING HIS TROOPS HOME WITH HIS SOMETIMES READY BATTERY...

What is an electric shock?

An electric shock is what you feel when electricity passes through your body. A strong shock can kill a person or cause painful burns. A fairly weak shock can sting your skin and make your muscles jerk.

Shocks are no fun. So here are a few "nevers" to remember. Never touch electrical things if they are wet, or if your hands are wet. And don't touch them if you are standing in a puddle or a bathtub. Water is a good conductor of electricity, so wetness increases your chances of getting a bad shock. Never climb telephone poles. And always keep away from any place that has a sign saying "Danger. High Voltage." This doesn't mean you should be afraid of electrical things. Just be very, very careful with them.

What is a power plant?

A power plant is a place where large amounts of electrical energy are generated.

There are at least seven different kinds of power plants. All of them have generators. But the power to run the generators comes from different things —steam, water, gas, or even wind.

The three most common kinds of plants are steam-turbine plants, hydro-electric (HY-droe-ih-LECK-tric) plants, and atomic or nuclear (NOO-klee-ur) plants.

682

How does a steam-turbine plant generate electricity?

A steam-turbine plant uses steam to spin the wheels of a turbine. The spinning motion of the turbine runs the generator that produces the electric current.

Steam is made by burning oil, coal, or gas to boil water. A huge amount of water is boiled. It makes a huge amount of steam. A steam-run plant is like a giant tea kettle with steam blowing out the spout. But instead of going through a spout, the steam goes through a tunnel. Inside the tunnel are wheels with blades. This tunnel full of blades is the turbine.

When steam blows through the tunnel, it makes the blades spin very fast. When the blades spin, the rod they are mounted on spins also. The rod is connected to the electric generators. When the rod spins, the generators run and produce electric currents.

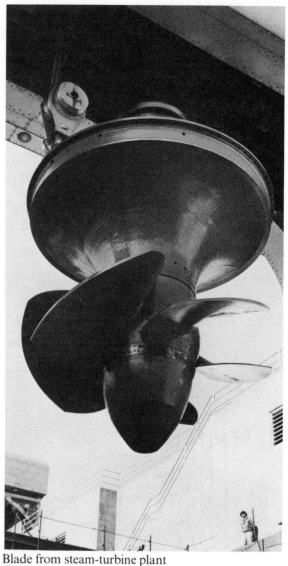

Blade from steam-turbine plant

How does a hydroelectric power plant generate electricity?

A hydroelectric power plant uses a water-powered turbine to run a generator. The water comes from a reservoir (REZ-ur-vwar) or a lake. Most of it is held back by a large wall called a dam. Gravity, the force that pulls everything downward, makes some water flow through tunnels from the top of the dam to the bottom. Just before the water is let out at the bottom of the dam, it runs through the turbines and makes them turn. Flowing water can turn turbines just as wind can turn windmills or pinwheels. When turbines turn, they make the generators turn, and electric currents are produced.

The world's largest power plant can make enough electrical energy to turn on 60 million 100-watt light bulbs.

683

What is a watt?

A watt is the unit used to measure electric power. A 100-watt light bulb uses 100 units of electrical energy every second. A 60-watt light bulb uses only 60 units of electrical energy every second. In either case, electrical energy is changed into heat and light energy. The watt is named after James Watt, the man who invented the steam engine.

How does an atomic power plant generate electricity?

An atomic power plant works almost the same as a steam-turbine power plant does. But an atomic plant doesn't burn coal, oil, or gas. Instead, it uses the metal uranium (you-RAY-nee-um) to make heat for boiling water. Instead of burning the uranium in a furnace, the uranium is put in a nuclear reactor. There, the atoms that make up the uranium split. And they produce huge amounts of nuclear energy. In doing this, a great amount of heat is given off. The heat turns water to steam. The steam blows through turbines, and the turbines turn the generators.

How does an electric current go from a power plant to people's houses?

It leaves the power plant through thick, heavy wires called transmission (tranz-MISH-un) lines. The current is sent out under high electrical pressure, or at high "voltage." The lines are held up off the ground by tall metal towers.

Transmission lines stretch for miles. When they come to a town where people need electricity, some of the lines go into a place called a substation. The substation changes the high-voltage electricity into low-voltage electricity, which is safer. The low-voltage electricity then goes through wires from the substation to a transformer. This makes the voltage even lower. From there it travels to houses, factories, and offices. In big cities, the wires carrying electricity to customers are in pipes or tunnels under the streets. In small towns, the wires are strung between wooden poles.

! The same person, Michael Faraday, invented the electric motor, the generator, and the transformer! !

What is a brownout?

Sometimes the area around a power plant needs more power than usual. This often happens in the summer when people are using air conditioners. Sometimes one power district can buy power from a neighboring power district. Special cables are set up to make this possible.

If your power district cannot buy enough from a neighbor, it may send out power to your home at lower voltage. This is called a brownout.

If the voltage is reduced just a little, you won't notice it. But if it is reduced 5 percent or more, your lights will be dimmer. And some appliances, such as your toaster and your iron, won't work as well as usual.

What is a blackout?

When the power plant stops sending electricity to your neighborhood, you have a blackout. The power company may do this purposely, in order to send more power to other areas during a shortage. Or, if something goes wrong at the power plant, there may be a blackout that nobody wants in a large area.

686

During a blackout, your street would be completely dark at night. You couldn't watch TV or listen to the radio or stereo (unless yours run on batteries). Your refrigerator would stop working. If you have an electric stove, your parents couldn't cook. You would have to do your homework by candlelight or flashlight!

WAM! WAM! WAM!

I REFUSE TO STAY OUT IN A BLACKOUT— IT'S A GOOD WAY TO GET MUGGED

What is an electric motor?

An electric motor is a kind of machine that is powered by electricity. The motor changes electric energy into movement that can do work. For example, an electric blender has a small motor inside it. When the blender is plugged in and the motor switch turned on, the motor starts to spin. It causes the blades inside the blender's large container to spin, too. The blades then can cut up any food you put in the container.

Why are electric wires covered with plastic or rubber?

The plastic or rubber insulates (IN-suh-lates) the wire. This means it keeps the electricity from leaking out through the sides of the wire. An insulated wire is safe to touch. A bare wire could shock or even kill someone who touches it. Sometimes when a wire is old, the insulation becomes cracked and starts to peel or break off. When this happens, someone might easily get a shock, or a fire might start. If you see a wire with cracked insulation, you should tell a grownup so that the wire can be replaced with a new one.

What makes a light go on when you flip a switch?

When you flip on a switch, you complete an electric circuit (SIR-kit). A circuit is like a closed loop. When electrons travel along a circuit, they eventually go back to the place where they started—as if they were going around in a circle. As long as the electrons keep flowing, the bulb stays lit. If you break the circuit, by cutting the wire or turning off the switch, the flow of electrons stops. Then the light goes out.

Open circuit

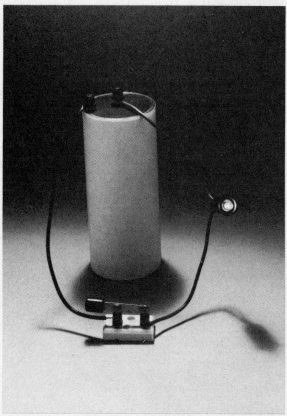

Closed circuit　　　　　Light bulb on

690

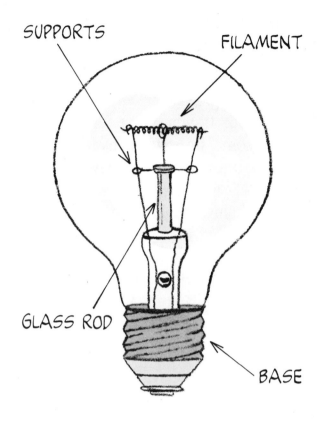

SUPPORTS

FILAMENT

GLASS ROD

BASE

What makes a light bulb light up?

Inside a light bulb is a thin wire called a filament (FILL-uh-munt). When electricity passes through the filament, the filament becomes very hot. It becomes so hot that it glows and gives off a bright white light. The glass part of a light bulb keeps air from reaching the filament. It is important to keep air away from the filament because air has oxygen (OCK-suh-jin) in it. Oxygen is one of the three things needed to start a fire. The other two are heat and something that can burn. A white-hot filament has the heat and is burnable. If any oxygen happened to reach a hot filament, it would burn up in an instant.

What makes light bulbs burn out?

When a light bulb stops working, we say that it has "burned" out. But it didn't really burn. What really happened was that the bulb's filament broke. When the filament breaks, electrons can't pass through it. When electrons can't pass through the filament, then the filament can't get white-hot and glow.

Heat is what makes the filament break. Heat causes tiny cracks to form in the filament. The more you use the bulb, the bigger the cracks become. Finally, one of the cracks will stretch all the way through the filament, and the filament will break apart.

SOME OF US CAN'T SLEEP WITHOUT A NIGHT LIGHT!

691

Who invented the electric light bulb?

Thomas Edison in 1879. He was one of the greatest inventors who ever lived. If you ask people to name some important inventors, usually the first one they will think of is Edison. His most famous inventions were the phonograph, the electric light bulb, and a motion-picture machine called a kinetoscope (kih-NEE-tuh-scope). All together he and his helpers invented over 1,000 things.

Thomas Alva Edison

 The oldest working light bulb has been burning in a firehouse in California since 1901!

What is the difference between a light bulb and a fluorescent lamp?

The most obvious difference is their shape. A light bulb usually has a pear shape. A fluorescent (flow-RESS-unt) lamp usually has a tube shape. But that is not all.

In a light bulb, light is made with a glowing hot filament. But in a fluorescent lamp, the glow comes from a special white coating on the inside of the glass tube. The coating glows whenever certain invisible rays, called ultraviolet (UL-truh-VYE-uh-lit) rays, hit it. These ultraviolet rays are made when you turn on the electricity. When the lamp is on, electrons shoot from one end of the tube to the other. The tube is filled with a special gas that gives off ultraviolet rays whenever electrons shoot through it. Fluorescent lamps help save money because they use much less electric power than light bulbs do.

692

What makes flash bulbs flash?

Oxygen. Flash bulbs have oxygen sealed inside. When you press the button on your camera, electric current flows through the bulb's filament. The filament glows. But the glow doesn't last the way it does in an ordinary light bulb. That is because the oxygen makes the filament burn up in a flash of bright light. This flash gives you a lot of light in enough time to snap a picture.

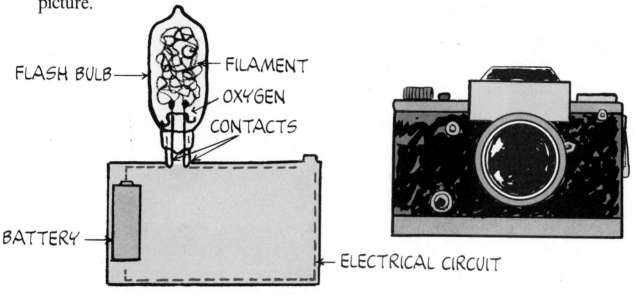

What makes toasters and electric irons get hot?

When a toaster or electric iron is turned on, an electric current flows through a coil of wire. This means that electrons are moving along among the atoms that make up the coil of the toaster or iron. As the electrons make their way, they bump into atoms. This bumping changes the energy of the current into heat energy. The coil becomes hot.

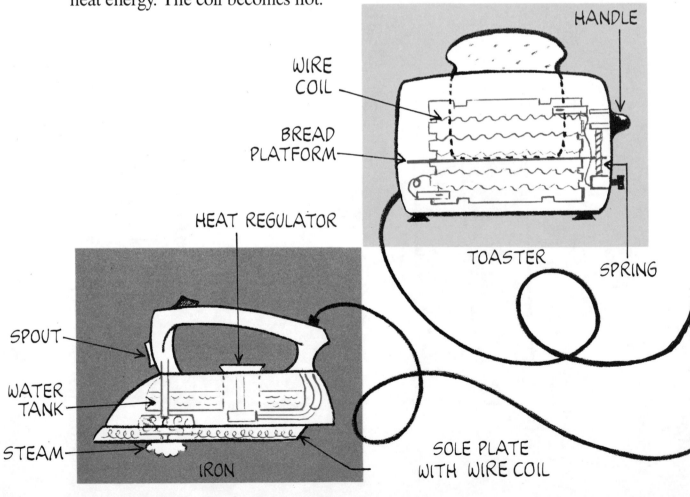

What does a fuse do?

It protects your house from fires caused by electricity. All electric current that comes into your house must pass through the fuse. If you take the fuse out, the circuit is broken. No electricity comes in. If you put the fuse back, your house has current again.

Inside the fuse is a piece of metal. If this piece of metal gets too hot, it melts very quickly. Melting is the way it protects your house.

For example, suppose you are using an air conditioner, a TV, an iron, and three lamps. Then you put on the toaster. You are now causing too much current to go through the circuit in your house. The wires become very hot and they could start a fire. However, before this can happen, the metal piece in the fuse melts from the heat. We say the fuse blew. Electrons can no longer flow through the wires of your house. So an electrical fire will not start.

In order to get electric current flowing into your house again, you must put in a new fuse. But first you have to shut off at least one appliance, such as the toaster or the iron. Then less current will be flowing through the wires in your house. The smaller current can be safely carried without blowing the fuse.

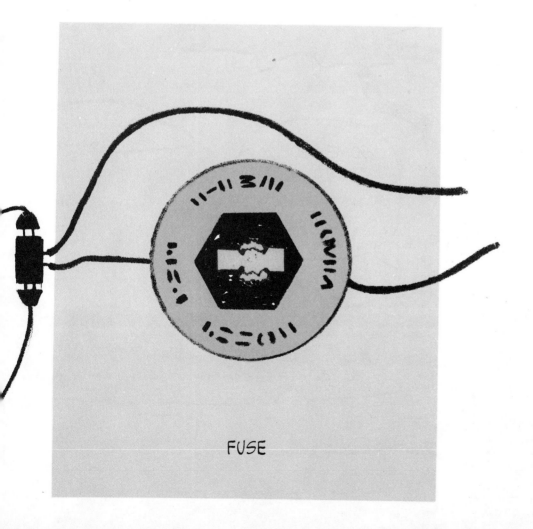

FUSE

Do circuits in all buildings have fuses?

No. Fuses are becoming old-fashioned. Newer buildings have circuit breakers instead. On the outside, circuit breakers look like ordinary light switches. But on the inside, a circuit breaker has a spring that bends when it gets hot. The spring will get hot if too much current is going through the circuit. If the spring gets hot and bends, the circuit breaker will flip to the off position. The current shuts off. After you wait a few minutes for the spring to cool, you can flip the circuit breaker back on. But before you do that, you should turn off some of your lights and appliances. Then the circuit breaker probably won't switch off again.

How does the electric company know how much to charge each customer?

Each customer's house or apartment has a meter that measures how much electric energy the customer uses. The numbers on the dial tell the company's meter reader how many kilowatt-hours of electrical energy the customer has used. A kilowatt is a unit of electric power. One kilowatt is equal to 1,000 watts. If you use a 1,000-watt iron for an hour, then you have used one kilowatt-hour of electricity. If you keep a 100-watt bulb burning for ten hours, that also adds up to one kilowatt-hour. The meter keeps track of every little bit of electrical energy that is used. And it all adds up to a certain number of kilowatt-hours.

697

Can electricity help people send messages?

Yes. If you want to contact someone far away, and you want to do it quickly, you must use a telegraph, a telephone, a radio, or maybe a television. All these methods use electrical energy.

What is a telegraph?

A telegraph is the oldest method of using electricity to send and receive messages. Samuel F. B. Morse invented the telegraph in 1837. For the first time people could contact each other instantly between any two places that could be connected by wires. Before the telegraph, messages had to be sent by mail or by private messenger. The telegraph is no longer used much. It has been replaced by telephones and radios.

How does a telegraph work?

Besides wires and batteries, a telegraph system has two main parts. One is a sender, called a key. The other is a receiver, called a sounder. The person working the telegraph is called the operator.

The key is really just a switch. The operator presses the key to make current flow through the wires. When the operator stops pressing, the current stops. The sounder has an electromagnet. When the current is on, the electromagnet moves a lever made of iron. When the lever moves, it goes "tap" or "click" against another piece of iron. Different patterns of clicks stand for different letters of the alphabet. The receiving operator listens to the clicks and can understand the message that the sending operator is spelling. This system of using clicks to stand for letters is called Morse code.

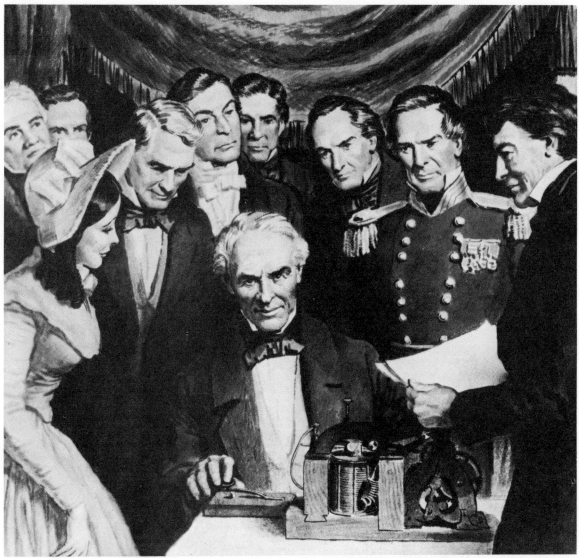

Samuel F. B. Morse sends the first telegram

Do people still use Morse code?

Not usually. But a code much like Morse's is still used by radio operators. Instead of clicks, the radio code uses short and long beeps, called dots and dashes. If you know someone who operates a radio as a hobby, maybe you can listen to people talking to each other in code. If you learn the code, you will be able to understand what they are saying.

Write your name here, using Morse code.

Can you read this?

Was there any fast way to send messages between America and Europe before telephones were invented?

Yes. In 1866 a heavy wire called a cable was laid across the bottom of the Atlantic Ocean. This cable made it possible for people to send telegraph messages between America and Europe. Before the cable was laid, messages had to go by ship. This meant that people didn't know what was happening on the other side of the ocean until days or weeks later.

Now there are cables under all the world's oceans. They carry telephone messages and other electric signals.

 The longest undersea cable runs about 9,000 miles (more than 14,000 kilometers), from Australia to Canada!

Cable on ocean floor

THAT'S TOO DEEP FOR ME.

GOOD GRIEF!

How does a telephone work?

Every time you talk, you start sound waves moving through the air. When you talk over the telephone to a friend, the sound waves from your voice enter the part of the phone called the mouthpiece. The sound waves flow against a paper-thin piece of metal called a diaphragm (DYE-uh-fram). They make it vibrate—move back and forth very quickly.

As the diaphragm vibrates, it jiggles tiny bits of carbon in a small box attached to it. The carbon bits bunch together or spread apart in time with the vibrations of your voice.

An electric current flows over the telephone wires between your house and your friend's house. The action of the carbon bits changes the strength of the electric current that goes over the wires. The current is strong when the carbon bits bunch together. It is weak when they spread apart. As a result, the spurts of current follow the same pattern as the sound waves from your voice.

When the spurts of current reach your friend's house, they must be changed back into the sound of your voice. In your friend's phone (and in yours too) is a small electromagnet. When the spurts of current reach the electromagnet, another thin metal diaphragm begins to vibrate. This diaphragm is in the part of the phone called the earpiece. The vibrations set sound waves in motion. The sound waves reach your friend's ears, and your friend hears you say "Hello!"

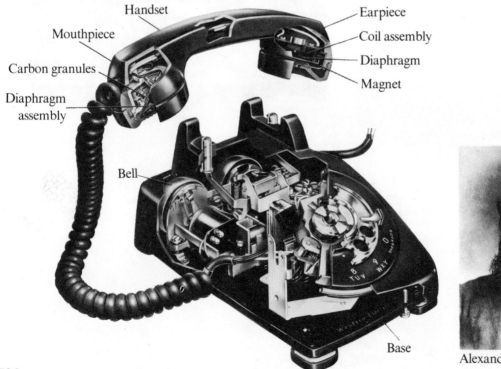

Handset

Mouthpiece

Carbon granules

Diaphragm assembly

Earpiece

Coil assembly

Diaphragm

Magnet

Bell

Base

Alexander Graham Bell

There are about 400 million telephones in the world! More than a third of them are in the United States!

HI, CHUCK? IT'S PEPPERMINT PATTY. YOU DIALED THE WRONG NUMBER... BUT THAT'S O.K.

 The average American makes about 1,000 telephone calls each year!

WILL YOU TWO GET OFF THE PHONE? THIS IS A PARTY LINE AND I'M STILL TALKING!

 Alexander Graham Bell invented the telephone while trying (without success) to invent a hearing aid for deaf people!

A PARTY... DID SHE SAY A PARTY? I'LL BE RIGHT OVER.

How does a radio work?

Radio is a way of sending voices and music through the air instead of along electric wires. It's like a wireless telephone. In fact, when radio was first invented, people called it the wireless. Instead of wires, radio uses electromagnetic waves. These waves can travel through air—and even through space.

704

How are radio waves made?

Radio waves are made by a transmitter with the help of an antenna. A transmitter is a radio sender. The set you listen to is a radio receiver. The radio programs you hear are sent out by transmitters from radio-broadcasting studios.

A transmitter makes an electric current that vibrates very fast. It vibrates many thousands or even millions of times a second. Such a fast vibrating current can flow through a wire like an ordinary current. But when it is sent through an antenna, it changes form. Out of the antenna comes an invisible electromagnetic field that reaches for miles. Sometimes it even reaches halfway around the earth. This field is made of radio waves. These waves can be picked up by a receiver.

What does an antenna look like?

An antenna can be a piece of wire. Or it may be a whole bunch of wires hanging like a net from tall towers. Sometimes an antenna may be a metal pole or rod sticking straight up. Other times it may be shaped like a dish. The type of antenna used depends on how fast the radio waves are vibrating, how far you want them to go, and in which direction you want them to go.

How do radio waves carry voices and music?

If you went into a radio station, you would see someone talking into a microphone or playing music on a phonograph. A microphone is much like the mouthpiece of a telephone. When you talk into it, sound waves cause a piece of metal in the microphone to vibrate. An electric current flows through the microphone. The current vibrates in time with the vibrations of voices or music. This current can travel only along wires. But the job of a radio station is to send this current out to radio receivers. The trick, then, is to get the microphone current to hitch a piggyback ride on the transmitter current. The combination can travel through the air or space as radio waves.

A radio transmitter has a part called a modulator (MOJ-uh-lay-tur). It mixes the microphone current with the transmitter current. In this way, the microphone vibrations can leave the antenna together with the transmitter's radio waves. That is how the sounds can be made to travel out through air and space.

Radio waves travel at about the
same speed as light (186,000 miles or
297,600 kilometers per second). There is nothing faster!

Can radio waves be sent in a straight beam?

Yes. Most antennas send out radio waves in all directions. To send the waves in a straight beam, you need a special antenna. This type of antenna is curved, like a dish. Radio waves come out in all directions from a rod pointing from the middle of the dish. Many of these waves then hit the curved part of the dish. The curve causes the waves to bounce back out away from the dish. Then they travel in a straight beam.

Can a dish-shaped antenna receive radio waves?

Yes. Like most antennas, dish-shaped antennas can receive as well as send. Some, like radar antennas, send and receive at the same time. Dish antennas are very good for communicating with space satellites. They can be aimed directly at a satellite, so that a clear, strong signal can be sent thousands of miles away. When receiving, a dish antenna picks up signals only from the direction in which it is aimed. The signal comes through very clearly.

Dish-shaped antenna

Who invented the radio?

Guglielmo (goo-lee-YELL-moh) Marconi (mar-KOE-nee) invented radio in 1895 when he was 21 years old. Marconi became very interested in science when he was a boy. He began doing experiments when he was 16. For a long time, scientists had said it should be possible to make a radio—or wireless telegraph, as it was called. But nobody could figure out how to do it. Marconi studied the other scientists' ideas and experiments. Then, when he was 20, he tried to invent a radio on his own. Finally he built a transmitter and a receiver. The transmitter could send telegraph messages across his attic without wires. But would it work over a long distance?

Marconi had his brother carry the receiver over a hill, far away out of sight. The brother also carried a rifle. Then Marconi used the transmitter to send a message to his brother. Marconi stopped and listened. Bang! He heard a rifle shot in the distance. It was his brother's signal that the message had been received. Marconi's invention was a success.

EXHIBITION OF INVENTORS

TODAY'S LECTURE STARTS AT 2 P.M. ON G. MARCONI

708

Early radio makers broadcast their own programs. If they hadn't, no one would have had a reason to buy a radio. There were no other programs to listen to!

How many radio-broadcasting stations are there?

The United States has about 8,000 radio-broadcasting stations.

Why don't the radio waves from different stations get mixed up in the air?

When you play your radio, you turn the dial to a number. The number may be 700 or 1100 or one of many other numbers. (There may be just a 7 or an 11 on your radio dial. If the radio is small, the zeros will be left out.) Each number stands for what is called a frequency (FREE-kwun-see). Each station broadcasts at a different frequency. The frequency is the rate of vibration of the waves that come from the station's transmitter. Your radio can "tune in" on the particular frequency you want to hear. Waves from other stations go by without being picked up.

 About half the radios in the world are in the United States!

What is a two-way radio?

A two-way radio is one that can send out radio signals and pick them up also. The radio you have in your house is a one-way radio. It only receives radio waves. The radio transmitter in a broadcasting station is also a one-way radio. It sends out radio waves.

A two-way radio is the kind you sometimes see taxicab drivers using. They talk into it to tell the cab company where they are taking you. They also get messages from the cab company through this radio.

People use two-way radios in boats, airplanes, police cars, and other places where it's not possible to have telephone wires.

711

What is a radio ham?

A radio ham has nothing to do with food. It is a person who sends and receives radio messages as a hobby. Many boys and girls become radio hams. They send messages to other hams by code or by voice. There are special frequencies set aside for them to use. In order to send messages, hams have to pass a test and get a license. They also must have special equipment—a transmitter, a receiver, and an antenna. Many hams build their own equipment from kits. If you want to become a ham, the equipment will cost you anywhere from fifty dollars to many thousands of dollars.

What is a CB radio?

CB stands for Citizens Band. It is a group of frequencies that is reserved for ordinary people to use. You do not need a license to use a CB radio. Usually, people have CB radios in their cars. Truck drivers use CB's a lot. They talk with other drivers and find out about traffic conditions.

A special language has grown up among CB users. It is a kind of code. For example, "Smoky" means policeman. "Rolling double nickels" means driving at 55 miles an hour.

How does black-and-white television work?

The screen that you look at is the front end of something called a picture tube. The screen is coated on the inside with a chemical that glows when it is hit by electrons. The electrons come from a part of the TV called an electron gun. It is in the back of the picture tube. If you look closely at the screen, you can see lots of thin lines running across it. The electron gun fires a row of electrons along each line. Some places on the line are hit by a lot of electrons, and they light up brightly. Other places are hit by fewer electrons. These places appear light gray, dark gray, or black. The darkness depends on how many electrons hit them. When you look at all the light and dark spots together, your eyes see a picture. It's like a black-and-white photograph in a newspaper. If you look closely at a newspaper photograph, you can see that it is made up of lots of tiny dots.

Electrons shoot out of electron gun

How does a picture get to your television set?

A picture gets to your TV in much the same way that sound reaches your radio. Radio waves carry the picture from a transmitting station, through the air, to your TV set.

715

How is it possible to see color on a TV?

Color television is very much like a comic strip or a color photograph printed in a magazine. The picture is a mixture of thousands and thousands of little colored dots (red, green, and blue). If you look at a color television screen very closely, you can see the little dots. When the set is off, the dots look gray or silvery. But when the set is on, the dots light up.

The dots are made of a chemical that glows when hit by a beam of electrons shot from an electron gun. A black-and-white television set has only one electron gun. But a color set has three, one for each color—red, green, and blue. Other colors—yellow, orange, purple, brown, black, or white—are made to appear on the screen by controlling how many red, green, and blue dots light up. For example, a picture of a glass of orange juice would be made of a large number of red dots and a smaller number of green dots. The tiny red, green, and blue dots mix together to form many colors.

A color television camera separates everything it looks at into red, green, or blue. Then, the television station transmits a red picture, a green picture, and a blue picture. The television set catches these pictures with its antenna and sends the pictures to the three electron guns. The three pictures are mixed on the screen to show the same colors as the camera saw.

716

Here you see how a magnet can make electrons move. The television screen has a black spot and a crooked picture because magnetism is bending the beams of electrons that shoot from the electron gun to the screen.

How does a phonograph record make sounds?

The surface of a record is covered with narrow circles that are very close together. If you look at those circles with a magnifying glass or a microscope, you will see that they are very wavy. When the record turns, the waves make the stylus—the phonograph needle—vibrate. The vibrations in the stylus cause vibrations in the strength of an electric current. The current goes to something called an amplifier. It makes the current stronger. Then, current from the amplifier makes a loudspeaker vibrate. And you hear the sound that was recorded.

What is a phonograph?

"Phonograph" is a word that is becoming very old-fashioned. People once used it to mean a record player or a hi-fi set. A modern phonograph is usually called a stereo.

What is hi-fi?

Hi-fi is short for high fidelity. Fidelity refers to how accurately a record or stereo set makes sounds. A high-fidelity recording of an orchestra should sound almost exactly like a real orchestra.

What does stereo mean?

Stereo means a sound-recording system that uses two or more microphones for recording and two or more loudspeakers for listening. The extra microphones and loudspeakers make the sound more realistic. With a stereo system, different sounds come from different loudspeakers. For example, you might hear a saxophone on one speaker and a guitar on the other. It would be just like having the musicians right in the same room with you. On a nonstereo phonograph, the guitar and saxophone sounds would be mixed together and come out of one speaker. Another word for nonstereo is monaural (mon-OR-ul), which means "one ear." Listening to a monaural record is almost like listening to live music with only one of your ears.

How does a tape recorder work?

A tape recorder works by magnetism. The tape is a plastic ribbon coated with a chemical called iron oxide. Each tiny bit, or particle, of iron oxide is like a little magnet.

Inside a tape recorder is an electromagnet called a recording head. When electric waves from a microphone go into the tape recorder, they cause vibrations in the field around the electromagnet. As the tape passes through the electromagnet's field, the bits of iron oxide on the tape are magnetized into different patterns.

When you play back the tape, the patterns on it affect another electromagnet called a playback head. This electromagnet makes waves that go into an amplifier. The amplifier makes the waves stronger. The strong waves make a loudspeaker vibrate. The sound vibrations that come from the speaker are just like the ones that went into the microphone.

Index